COMPLETE GUIDE TO SHEEP FARMING

Mastering Sustainable Practices, Breeding Techniques, And Profit Strategies For Successful Wool And Meat Production

GIOVANNI MALAKAI

© [2024] [Giovanni Malakai]. All rights reserved.

Except for brief quotations included in critical reviews and certain other noncommercial uses allowed by copyright law, no part of this publication may be reproduced, distributed, or transmitted in any form or by any means, including photocopying, recording, or other electronic or mechanical methods, without the publisher's prior written permission. Write to the publisher at the address below, addressing your letter to the "Attention: Permissions Coordinator," requesting permission.

DISCLAIMER

This book's content is solely intended for informational and educational purposes. The author and publisher of this book make no express or implied representations or warranties of any kind regarding the completeness, accuracy, reliability, suitability, or availability of the information, products, services, or related graphics contained in it, even though every effort has been made to ensure their accuracy and dependability. You consequently absolutely assume all risk associated with any reliance you may have on such material.

The author's own experiences and studies serve as the foundation for the techniques and procedures covered in this book. They might not be appropriate for every circumstance or person. Before putting any advice or recommendations from this book into practice, readers should use their own discretion and take into account their unique situation. Consulting with qualified professionals who specialize in veterinary care and animal management is always a good idea. Any direct, indirect, incidental or consequential damages resulting from using or relying on the material in this book are disclaimed by the author and publisher. Any decisions made by the reader based on the information presented herein are at their own risk.

TABLE OF CONTENTS

CHAPTER ONE 13
INTRODUCTION TO SHEEP FARMING 13
- KNOWING THE FUNDAMENTALS OF SHEEP FARMING 13
- THE ADVANTAGES AND DIFFICULTIES OF SHEEP FARMING...............14
- ESSENTIAL KNOWLEDGE AND SKILL SET NEEDED 15
- THE VALUE OF APPROPRIATE MANAGEMENT AND PLANNING.........16
- AN OVERVIEW OF THE FEATURES OF SHEEP BREEDS 17

CHAPTER TWO 19
BEGINNING..19
- RECOGNIZING THE FUNDAMENTALS OF SHEEP FARMING 19
- THE ADVANTAGES AND DIFFICULTIES OF SHEEP FARMING...............20
- KEY INFORMATION AND SKILL SET NEEDED........................22
- THE VALUE OF APPROPRIATE MANAGEMENT AND PLANNING.........24
- A SYNOPSIS OF SHEEP BREEDS AND THEIR FEATURES 25

CHAPTER THREE 27
FEEDING AND NUTRITION OF SHEEP 27
- RECOGNIZING NUTRITIONAL REQUIREMENTS AT VARIOUS STAGES.27
- CHOOSING HIGH-QUALITY SUPPLEMENTS AND FEEDS......28
- PUTTING SUITABLE FEEDING PROCEDURES IN PLACE........30
- HANDLING THE ROTATION OF PASTURE AND GRAZING ...31
- TAKING CARE OF TYPICAL NUTRITIONAL ISSUES................33

CHAPTER FOUR 35
MANAGEMENT OF HEALTH AND DISEASE 35
- PUTTING PREVENTIVE HEALTH MEASURES INTO PRACTICE 35

    RECOGNIZING TYPICAL ILLNESSES AND PARASITES 36

    GIVING MEDICATION AND VACCINATIONS...37

    CREATING A SYSTEM FOR MONITORING HEALTH................................38

    SPEAKING WITH EXPERTS IN VETERINARY MEDICINE 39

CHAPTER FIVE..41

  REPRODUCTION AND BREEDING...41

    RECOGNIZING THE REPRODUCTIVE CYCLES OF SHEEP......................41

    CHOOSING GENETICS AND BREEDING STOCK 42

    PUTTING BREEDING PROGRAMS IN PLACE 43

    HANDLING THE LAMBING AND PREGNANCY 44

    TAKING CARE OF REPRODUCTIVE ISSUES..45

CHAPTER SIX...47

  ACCOMMODATIONS AND AMENITIES 47

    CREATING USABLE AND EFFECTIVE HOUSING STRUCTURES.............47

    PROVIDING SUFFICIENT AIR AND SHELTER 48

    MAINTAINING HYGIENE AND CLEANLINESS.......................................49

    HANDLING TRASH AND ITS EFFECT ON THE ENVIRONMENT 51

    PUTTING SAFETY PROCEDURES IN PLACE FOR HANDLERS AND 52

CHAPTER SEVEN 55

  PRACTICES FOR FLOCK MANAGEMENT...55

    CREATING EFFICIENT DOCUMENTATION SYSTEMS............................55

    PUTTING GRAZING AND ROTATION STRATEGIES INTO PRACTICE 56

    SURVEILLING AND CONTROLLING FLOCK BEHAVIOR 57

    RECOGNIZING AND RESOLVING PROBLEMS WITH SOCIAL 58

    ORGANIZING FOR WEATHER AND SEASONAL CHANGES 59

CHAPTER EIGHT 61
STRATEGIES FOR MARKETING AND SALES 61
RECOGNIZING DEMAND AND MARKET TRENDS 61
CREATING A UNIQUE BRAND IDENTITY FOR YOUR ITEMS 62
INVESTIGATING SALES AND MARKETING CHANNELS........................ 64
COST ANALYSIS AND PRICING STRATEGIES 65
DEVELOPING LOYALTY AND RELATIONSHIPS WITH CUSTOMERS 67
CHAPTER NINE 69
MONEY HANDLING.. 69
SETTING ASIDE MONEY FOR STARTUP AND ONGOING EXPENSES..... 69
MONITORING REVENUE AND EXPENSES.. 70
PUTTING RISK MANAGEMENT AND FINANCIAL CONTROLS IN 71
LOOKING FOR INVESTMENT AND FINANCING POSSIBILITIES............. 73
ORGANIZING FOR FINANCIAL SUSTAINABILITY OVER THE LONG........ 74
CHAPTER TEN 77
SUSTAINABILITY OF THE ENVIRONMENT 77
PUTTING SUSTAINABLE FARMING PRACTICES INTO PRACTICE.......... 77
EFFECTIVELY MANAGING RESOURCES (WATER, ENERGY, ETC.) 78
ENCOURAGING ECOSYSTEM HEALTH AND BIODIVERSITY 79
TAKING ON THE CHALLENGES OF CLIMATE CHANGE........................ 80
TAKING PART IN CONSERVATION PROGRAMS................................. 81
CHAPTER ELEVEN 83
UPCOMING DEVELOPMENTS AND TRENDS 83
EXAMINING THE USE OF TECHNOLOGY IN SHEEP FARMING 83
USING ORGANIC AND SUSTAINABLE PRACTICES............................... 84

MONITORING INNOVATIONS AND INDUSTRY TRENDS 86
PROSPECTS FOR GROWTH AND DIVERSIFICATION 87
ONGOING EDUCATION AND TALENT ACQUISITION 89

ABOUT THE BOOK

Anyone stepping foot in the exciting world of sheep husbandry should consult the "Complete Guide to Sheep Farming". It dives deeply into the complexities of this sector, providing insightful information on all facets, from the fundamentals to the newest developments and trends.

It is essential to comprehend the fundamentals of sheep farming, and this guide thoroughly addresses the Rewards and Difficulties of this fulfilling pursuit. It highlights the necessary knowledge and skills and stresses how crucial effective planning and management are to success.

Making important choices while starting a sheep farm includes choosing the appropriate location, putting up a sufficient infrastructure, and obtaining high-quality breeding stock. Each stage, including managing regulatory and legal requirements and creating a comprehensive business plan to guarantee a strong foundation, is painstakingly detailed in the guide.

Fundamental elements that have a direct impact on flock health and productivity are feeding and nutrition for sheep. This manual provides information on managing pasture rotation and grazing, choosing high-quality feeds, and addressing common nutritional concerns. It also teaches readers how to understand nutritional needs.

Maintaining a healthy flock depends critically on managing health and disease. The handbook offers information on Vaccination Protocols, Disease Identification, Preventive Health Measures, and building a strong Health Monitoring System in conjunction with Veterinary Professionals.

Strategies for breeding and reproduction are essential for the genetic advancement and sustainability of flocks. Sheep reproductive cycles, breeding stock selection, breeding programs, pregnancy and lambing management, and methods for dealing with reproductive challenges are all explained in this guide.

For the comfort and well-being of the flock, housing and facilities are essential. Designing functional housing structures, offering sufficient shelter and ventilation, upholding cleanliness and hygiene, managing waste, and putting safety precautions in place for livestock and handlers are all covered in the guide.

Operational efficiency depends on the use of effective flock management practices. To adjust to weather circumstances, this guide provides advice on record-keeping systems, grazing strategies, flock behavior monitoring, social hierarchy management, and seasonal planning.

Strategies for sales and marketing are essential for business success. Understanding market trends, creating a brand identity, investigating marketing channels, developing pricing strategies, and cultivating long-term customer relationships are all covered in detail in this guide.

To be sustainable, financial management is essential. For a successful sheep farming business, the guide covers financial controls, risk management, budgeting, expense tracking, funding opportunities, and long-term financial planning.

Concern for environmental sustainability is growing. The handbook promotes resource management, biodiversity promotion, climate change adaptation, sustainable farming practices, and active involvement in conservation initiatives.

To keep ahead of the curve in this fast-paced industry, future trends and innovations in sheep farming are examined. These include technology integration, sustainable practices, industry trends, opportunities for diversification, and continuous learning.

CHAPTER ONE

INTRODUCTION TO SHEEP FARMING

KNOWING THE FUNDAMENTALS OF SHEEP FARMING

Raising sheep for various uses, such as meat, wool, and milk, is the centuries-old agricultural activity known as sheep farming, or sheep husbandry. You need a suitable location with enough pastureland, shelter, and fence before you can begin sheep farming. To keep the sheep confined to approved areas and deter predators, proper fencing is essential. It's critical to comprehend sheep's natural behavior since they are gregarious, flock-oriented creatures that need constant observation to ensure their health and welfare.

A few essential duties in sheep farming are feeding, watering, and giving medical attention to the animals. Understanding sheep's dietary requirements, which change depending on their age, breed, and reproductive state, is essential while feeding them. For the health and productivity of sheep, clean water is essential. A healthy flock must be maintained by regular deworming, immunizations, and health examinations. Another crucial step in producing wool is shearing sheep, which is usually done once a year to collect wool without endangering the animals.

THE ADVANTAGES AND DIFFICULTIES OF SHEEP FARMING

A few advantages of sheep farming include a variety of revenue streams from the sale of meat, wool, and other byproducts like milk and hides. Sheep require less area and feed than other livestock, making them comparatively low-maintenance animals. By grazing on pasturelands, they also contribute to sustainable agriculture by controlling vegetation and enhancing soil health. For people who are enthusiastic about animal husbandry and environmentally friendly farming methods, sheep farming can also be a rewarding way of life.

Sheep husbandry does, however, present several difficulties. If appropriate precautions are not taken, predation by wolves, coyotes, and other predators can result in large losses. To prevent outbreaks and preserve flock health, disease management, and parasite control require routine monitoring and action. Profitability can be impacted by shifts in the market and customer preferences, therefore sheep producers must keep up with industry developments and modify their business plans as necessary.

ESSENTIAL KNOWLEDGE AND SKILL SET NEEDED

A variety of abilities and expertise are necessary for successful sheep farming. It is essential to comprehend animal behavior and fundamental veterinary care to quickly detect and treat health problems. Understanding nutrition and managing pastures contributes to the best use of feed supplies and the upkeep of grazing areas. Farmers who are proficient in breeding and reproduction practices can efficiently control breeding seasons and gradually enhance flock genetics.

To manage finances, marketing, and record-keeping, sheep farmers should also possess business management abilities. Having strong networking and communication abilities is essential for establishing connections with suppliers, customers, and other farmers. Long-term success in sheep farming requires lifelong learning and keeping up with industry innovations, such as new technologies for flock management or sustainable farming methods.

THE VALUE OF APPROPRIATE MANAGEMENT AND PLANNING

Succeeding in sheep farming requires careful planning and management. Farmers should create a thorough business strategy before they begin, including objectives, spending plans, schedules, and risk control techniques. Strategic planning includes selecting the appropriate sheep breeds based on production objectives, climate appropriateness, and market demand.

Sufficient facilities, like as equipment, handling areas, and shelters, must be established to facilitate productive agricultural activities.

Monitoring flock health, nutrition, and reproductive cycles regularly is one of the most effective management techniques. By putting biosecurity procedures into place, farms can stop the spread of illness and preserve their biosecurity. Proactive management requires timely immunizations, breeding programs, and parasite control measures. The overall resilience and sustainability of a sheep farming operation are also influenced by marketing strategy, emergency plans, and financial management.

AN OVERVIEW OF THE FEATURES OF SHEEP BREEDS

The size, quality of the wool, amount of meat produced, and climate tolerance of different breeds of sheep vary greatly. The popular meat breeds Hampshire, Dorset, and Suffolk are prized for their quick growth and excellent meat. Breeds with two purposes, like Corriedale and Columbia, can provide wool as well as meat. High-end textiles and clothing can be made from the fine wool that Merino sheep are known for.

Because of their long, dense fleeces, breeds like Targhee, Lincoln, and Rambouillet are preferred for producing wool. Breeds of hair sheep like the Katahdin and Dorper require less upkeep and shearing because they naturally shed their wool. Regional and historical breeds frequently possess distinctive qualities that make them ideal for particular settings or customary agricultural methods. When choosing and maintaining their flocks for maximum productivity and profitability, farmers may make more informed decisions if they are aware of the traits of the various sheep breeds.

CHAPTER TWO

BEGINNING

RECOGNIZING THE FUNDAMENTALS OF SHEEP FARMING

Sheep farming is a lucrative endeavor, but success demands a solid grasp of the fundamentals. Understanding the many sheep species and their traits is one of the essential components. Understanding the different breeds—like the Merino, Suffolk, and Dorset—and how they differ in terms of meat output, wool quality, and climatic adaptation is part of this. Additionally, as it affects management strategies and farm productivity overall, understanding the sheep lifecycle—from lambing to market readiness—is essential.

Moreover, understanding sheep's nutritional requirements is critical to their development and well-being. Since they are mainly herbivores, sheep need a diet rich in grass, hay, grains, and supplements like vitamins and minerals.

Comprehending their dietary needs contributes to preserving their health and maximizing their output. Additionally, maintaining the flock's well-being and reducing disease-related losses depend heavily on understanding prevalent health problems and how to avoid and treat them.

Last but not least, establishing a favorable environment for the animals requires familiarity with the infrastructure required for sheep farming. This involves having enough fencing to keep the flock contained and keep predators out, appropriate housing or shelters to protect against inclement weather, and appropriate handling facilities for chores like shearing, vaccinating, and deworming. In general, having a firm understanding of these fundamentals lays the groundwork for a prosperous sheep farming enterprise.

THE ADVANTAGES AND DIFFICULTIES OF SHEEP FARMING

Sheep farming is a lucrative endeavor for farmers due to its numerous advantages. The several revenue streams it offers are among its main benefits. Raising sheep can result in multiple income streams since they can be raised for milk, meat, and wool. Because of its flavor and tenderness, lamb is a popular option among consumers, while wool in particular is in constant demand in the textile industry. Sheep are useful for managing pastures and conserving land because of their effective grazing practices.

But there are additional difficulties associated with raising sheep, which farmers must deal with. Predator control is a major concern since sheep are susceptible to attacks by wolves, coyotes, and foxes. Protecting the flock requires putting in place efficient fences and predator deterrents like guard dogs or electric fencing. To prevent serious losses, it's also important to manage sheep health and prevent diseases like foot rot or parasites through regular monitoring and appropriate veterinarian care.

Price volatility and market swings present another difficulty, particularly for goods made of wool and beef.

To optimize profitability, farmers must remain up to date on market trends, demand-supply dynamics, and pricing tactics. Furthermore, seasonal fluctuations in the quality and availability of feed can affect the nutrition and production of sheep, requiring year-round careful planning and management. Successful sheep producers can benefit from a profitable and sustainable business despite these obstacles.

KEY INFORMATION AND SKILL SET NEEDED

Farmers must acquire the necessary abilities and information about agricultural methods and animal management to succeed in sheep farming. Animal husbandry, which includes managing sheep's reproductive system, handling methods, and behavior, is an essential skill.

This covers knowledge of appropriate feeding practices, breeding tactics, helping with lambing, and identifying symptoms of illness or distress in sheep. Gaining these abilities guarantees the flock's best care and welfare.

Additionally, maintaining a productive and healthy sheep farm requires an understanding of feed production and pasture management. This entails being aware of weed control, pasture rotation, soil fertility, and grazing systems designed with sheep's dietary requirements in mind.

In addition to giving sheep high-quality feed, good pasture management improves soil health and promotes environmental sustainability.

Furthermore, managing finances effectively is crucial to the profitability of a sheep farming enterprise. This covers risk management, record-keeping, pricing strategies, cost analysis, and budgeting.

Financially astute farmers are better equipped to plan, make well-informed decisions, and maximize resource utilization for optimal profitability. All things considered, obtaining these abilities and know-how puts farmers on the right track for success in sheep farming.

THE VALUE OF APPROPRIATE MANAGEMENT AND PLANNING

A sheep farming business's capacity to succeed and last depends on careful planning and management. A well-written business plan functions as a road map, defining the aims, plans, tactics, and deadlines for different farming operations. This includes planning for upfront costs such as building supplies, machinery, buying livestock, and ongoing costs like labor, feed, and medical care.

All facets of farm operations, from flock management to financial administration, are covered by effective management techniques. This entails keeping thorough records of all financial transactions, health information, breeding histories, and sheep inventories.

Farmers are better equipped to make data-driven decisions and make necessary modifications when strengths, weaknesses, opportunities, and threats are identified through regular monitoring and evaluation of performance metrics.

Moreover, risk management techniques are essential for reducing unknowns and possible hazards in sheep farming. This includes liability, property, and livestock insurance as well as emergency plans for things like disease outbreaks, natural disasters, and market downturns. Putting sound agricultural practices and biosecurity measures into practice also helps to reduce risk and maintain the sustainability of farms. All things considered, sound planning and administration are essential cornerstones of a robust and prosperous sheep-farming enterprise.

A SYNOPSIS OF SHEEP BREEDS AND THEIR FEATURES

Numerous breeds of sheep are raised for diverse purposes, and each has its special qualities. Farmers can make well-informed decisions about breeding, management, and market targeting by having a thorough understanding of the many qualities exhibited by sheep breeds. The Merino sheep is a popular breed that is well-known for producing wool of exceptional quality and being able to adapt to a variety of conditions. Merinos are valuable to the textile industry because of their fine wool fibers, which are highly sought after.

The Suffolk sheep is another well-liked breed, valued for its high-quality meat and quick growth rates. Suffolks are well-known for having a powerful physique and a high feed conversion efficiency, which makes them perfect for producing meat. On the other hand, ewes of the popular Dorset sheep breed frequently give birth to several lambs during the lambing season. Because of their early maturity, milk production, and maternal instincts, dogs are prized for their suitability as meat and breeding animals.

Furthermore, several breeds—like the Romney and Border Leicester—are bred for certain markets or agricultural requirements and have unique qualities like longer wool fibers or better grazing capabilities.

CHAPTER THREE

FEEDING AND NUTRITION OF SHEEP

RECOGNIZING NUTRITIONAL REQUIREMENTS AT VARIOUS STAGES

Successful sheep husbandry requires an understanding of the nutritional requirements of sheep at different stages of life. For instance, a meal high in protein and energy is necessary to support the rapid growth and development of lambs. This can be accomplished by feeding premium ewe milk or milk substitutes together with creep feeds to promote early consumption of solid food. To facilitate healthy weight gain and skeletal development, lambs' diets should progressively change as they go from being weaned to being fed more roughage and balanced concentrates.

Depending on their physiological condition, adult sheep—ewes or rams—have different nutritional needs. To sustain fetal growth, pregnant ewes must consume enough protein and energy, particularly during the last trimester when the fetus develops quickly.

Mineral supplements like as calcium, phosphorus, and magnesium must be taken in the right amounts to avoid deficiencies and guarantee the health of the progeny. Conversely, a diet rich in nutrients is necessary for lactating ewes to support milk production and preserve their bodily condition.

Because of changes in metabolism and oral health, older sheep, especially aging ewes and rams, may require differing nutritional requirements. Softer meals or haylage could be necessary for them to facilitate chewing and digestion. To maximize sheep productivity and health, meals must be modified according to age and life stage. This way, every animal will get the nutrition it requires for healthy growth, reproduction, and general well-being.

CHOOSING HIGH-QUALITY SUPPLEMENTS AND FEEDS

Meeting the dietary needs of sheep requires a careful selection of premium feeds and supplements. Staple forages that are high in fiber, protein, and energy include hay, pasture grass, and silage. To guarantee the best possible health for sheep, aspects including nutrient content, maturity at harvest, and the lack of pollutants or mold should be taken into account while selecting hay or silage.

Supplements are essential for boosting some areas of sheep nutrition or correcting shortages in certain nutrients. Alfalfa pellets or soybean meal are examples of protein supplements that can increase protein intake, particularly in diets with insufficient protein sources. Mineral supplements can help prevent deficits and preserve general health. One example of a supplement is salt blocks that have been fortified with critical minerals like calcium, phosphorus, and trace elements.

Farmers can choose the best feeds and supplements for their flock's unique requirements by conducting feeding trials and consulting with nutritionists or veterinarians. Sheep are given a balanced diet for growth, reproduction, and general vigor when feed quality, nutritional content, and intake levels are regularly evaluated.

PUTTING SUITABLE FEEDING PROCEDURES IN PLACE

Optimizing the health and productivity of sheep requires the use of appropriate feeding methods. Digestion, nutrition absorption, and general health need to have adequate access to clean water. To avoid health problems, water sources should be constantly checked and kept clean.

Feeding schedules must be regular and customized to satisfy the dietary requirements of the flock's various groupings. Lambs may need longer feeding intervals to guarantee proper nutritional intake for growth, particularly in the early stages.

All year long, ewes and rams should have access to a balanced diet, with modifications made for breeding, gestation, and nursing.

To reduce waste and guarantee equitable access for all sheep, feeders, and troughs should be built to discourage rivalry and hostility during feeding periods. Feeds and supplements should be stored correctly to maintain nutritional quality and avoid contamination or spoiling in dry, clean settings.

Sheep producers may maximize nutrient intake, encourage healthy growth and reproduction, and improve flock performance by putting these recommended feeding strategies into effect.

HANDLING THE ROTATION OF PASTURE AND GRAZING

Optimizing fodder consumption and practicing sustainable sheep husbandry requires careful management of grazing and pasture rotation. Sheep are rotated between smaller paddocks or plots within pastures at regular intervals as part of rotational grazing. This method lowers parasite loads, preserves pasture quality, and permits grass to regenerate in rested regions.

Evaluating soil fertility and pasture health is the first step toward effective pasture management. To help farmers apply the right fertilizers or soil amendments to increase the quality of their fodder, soil testing helps identify pH and nutrient levels in the soil. To avoid overgrazing and soil erosion, pasture rotation programs should take seasonal growth patterns, weather, and stocking rates into account.

Grazing systems can be modified to meet the dietary requirements of various sheep species. Rich, quality grasslands may be beneficial for lambs and lactation ewes, but mature ewes and rams can do well on food that is older and has less protein. Consistent nutritional intake is ensured by supplementing at times when pasture supplies are limited or of low quality.

Decisions about grazing management tactics are influenced by routine monitoring of the state of the pasture, the availability of forage, and the grazing patterns of sheep. Farmers may improve forage consumption, promote healthy sheep production, and manage their property sustainably by putting into practice appropriate grazing and pasture rotation strategies.

TAKING CARE OF TYPICAL NUTRITIONAL ISSUES

It is imperative to attend to prevalent dietary issues to sustain ideal sheep health and yield. Mineral deficiencies are one prevalent concern that can result in health issues like poor growth, decreased fertility, and metabolic disorders. By giving sheep specialized mineral supplements based on forage and soil analysis, deficiency can be avoided and general health is promoted.

Inadequate protein consumption is another issue, particularly during times of increased demand like pregnancy, lactation, or rapid development. Sheep can be guaranteed to get enough protein for immune system development, muscle growth, and milk production by supplementing with high-protein diets such as alfalfa pellets, legume hay, or soybean meal.

Given that sheep are prone to digestive issues like bloat and acidity, digestive health is also very important. Gut health can be preserved and digestive problems can be avoided with proper forage management, which includes preventing abrupt changes in feed type or quantity, providing access to fresh water, and gradually introducing new pastures or diets to animals.

Fecal egg counts, veterinary evaluations, and routine body condition scores help farmers identify and quickly address nutritional issues in sheep. It could be essential to make modifications to feeding schedules, supplementation plans, or grazing management techniques to maximize nutrient intake and treat particular nutritional issues the flock is experiencing.

CHAPTER FOUR

MANAGEMENT OF HEALTH AND DISEASE

PUTTING PREVENTIVE HEALTH MEASURES INTO PRACTICE

Sustaining your sheep's health is essential to profitable husbandry. Keeping your flock healthy and disease-free is the goal of preventive health measures, which include a variety of procedures. Keeping your sheep in a clean and sanitary environment is an essential component. This includes giving pens a regular cleaning, making sure there is enough ventilation, and providing enough room for grazing and exercise. Adopting a stringent biosecurity plan also aids in preventing the spread of illnesses within your flock. This entails limiting who has access to your property, putting new animals in quarantine before bringing them into the flock, and routinely cleaning your cars and equipment.

Making sure your sheep are getting enough food is another essential preventive strategy. To keep their immune system and general health strong, they must eat a diet rich in important nutrients and well-balanced. This entails giving them constant access to fresh water, providing high-quality fodder and extra feed as needed, and keeping an eye on their dietary intake to avoid excesses or shortages. A licensed veterinarian's routine health examinations are also crucial for identifying and treating any possible health problems in their early stages.

RECOGNIZING TYPICAL ILLNESSES AND PARASITES

Effective disease management in sheep requires knowledge of common illnesses and parasites. Foot rot, pneumonia, enterotoxemia, and parasitic infections like worms are a few prevalent illnesses. Early detection of the symptoms of these illnesses can stop them from spreading and seriously endangering your flock. Fecal testing, behavior, and appearance observations, and routine health inspections are crucial for detecting any possible health problems in sheep.

Another issue in sheep husbandry is parasites, particularly roundworms, tapeworms, and lice.

Controlling parasite infestations can be achieved by following your veterinarian's advice for a deworming plan. Additionally, the danger of parasite transmission is decreased by maintaining clean bedding and rotating grazing sites as part of proper pasture management practices.

It is possible to intervene and treat sheep promptly when symptoms of parasite infestation, including weight loss, poor coat quality, and behavioral changes, are closely observed.

GIVING MEDICATION AND VACCINATIONS

Medication and vaccinations are essential for both illness prevention and treatment in sheep. Maintaining the immunization regimen that your veterinarian has prescribed will help shield your flock against common infectious diseases including respiratory infections, reproductive disorders, and clostridial diseases. Giving your sheep the necessary vaccinations at the right time will provide them with the best possible protection.

Furthermore, the well-being of sheep depends on giving them the appropriate medical attention when they are ill or injured.

Medication administration, including dewormers, antibiotics, and analgesics, should always be carried out in compliance with veterinarian advice and dosage guidelines. Drug resistance and health issues in sheep can result from overusing or misusing drugs. Maintaining thorough records of all immunizations and drugs given to your flock makes it easier to monitor their medical history and guarantees prompt follow-ups when needed. For efficient illness management, speaking with a veterinarian about any medication-related issues or treatment strategies is advised.

CREATING A SYSTEM FOR MONITORING HEALTH

Building a strong health monitoring system is essential to managing diseases on your sheep farm in a proactive manner. This entails conducting routine health examinations for every sheep, keeping an eye on body condition ratings, and documenting variations in weight over time. By keeping track of and evaluating these health indicators, it is possible to spot any changes from the usual state of health and take prompt action.

An extensive health monitoring system also includes the implementation of a quarantine policy for newly acquired animals. This entails keeping recent arrivals apart from the main flock for a predetermined amount of time to look for any indications of disease or illness. Monitoring for lameness, respiratory distress, odd behavior, and changes in appetite regularly can help identify health problems that need to be addressed. Developing and refining your health monitoring techniques in conjunction with a veterinarian will provide comprehensive and efficient disease surveillance on your farm.

SPEAKING WITH EXPERTS IN VETERINARY MEDICINE

Working together with veterinary specialists is essential to keeping your flock of sheep healthy and managing disease.

When it comes to giving knowledgeable advice on immunization schedules, drug administration, disease preventive techniques, and health monitoring procedures, veterinarians are essential. Having regular meetings with veterinarians enables you to monitor the health state of your flock and take preventative action when necessary.

Building a strong working relationship with your veterinarian guarantees access to prompt advice and emergency care should unforeseen health issues develop, in addition to routine veterinary appointments. Moreover, blood work, fecal examinations, and tissue samples are diagnostic tests that veterinarians can perform to precisely identify and treat illnesses in your sheep. Their knowledge and proficiency in managing the health of sheep are priceless resources for guaranteeing the welfare and output of your flock.

CHAPTER FIVE

REPRODUCTION AND BREEDING

RECOGNIZING THE REPRODUCTIVE CYCLES OF SHEEP

Understanding the reproductive cycles of sheep is essential for effective sheep management. The anoestrus, proestrus, oestrus, and metoestrus are the four main phases of these cycles. Anoestrus, which occurs when there is less sunshine throughout the winter, is a time when reproduction is inactive. The onset of proestrus, when ewes begin to exhibit signs of heat such as restlessness and increased vocalization, signals the start of the breeding season. Oestrus, which lasts for about 24 to 36 hours, is the true heat phase when ewes are open to mating. After oestrus, the ewe's reproductive system undergoes metestrus, when it either becomes ready for pregnancy or reverts to a non-pregnant state.

Farmers need to be skilled at identifying these periods and timing mating appropriately to enhance breeding success. Correctly identifying oestrus is aided by keeping an eye out for heat-related symptoms in sheep, such as enlarged vulvas and clear mucus discharge. To help with more accurate heat cycle detection, teaser rams, and ram marking harnesses can be used. Comprehending the time of these cycles guarantees effective breeding and maximum rates of lambing for a profitable sheep enterprise.

CHOOSING GENETICS AND BREEDING STOCK

The selection of appropriate genetics and breeding stock is critical to the success of any sheep farming endeavor. Breed choice is influenced by several variables, such as production objectives, market demand, and climate. Popular varieties for meat production, including Texel, Dorset, and Suffolk, are valued for their quick growth and high-quality meat, whereas breeds that produce excellent wool are Merino and Rambouillet. Combining favorable qualities from several breeds to increase overall output is known as crossbreeding, which can also be advantageous.

Consider factors including illness resistance, conformation, fertility, and mothering skills when selecting breeding stock. The best sheep for breeding are those in good health, with documented reproductive history and good body condition scores. Rams should have good structural conformation, high growth rates, and attractive carcass features, all of which are indications of outstanding genetics. A more profitable sheep business can be achieved by selecting superior breeding animals with the help of genetic testing and performance records, which guarantee genetic progress over generations.

PUTTING BREEDING PROGRAMS IN PLACE

In sheep farming, putting into practice efficient breeding plans is crucial to attaining targeted production results. Reproductive technologies, genetic management, and strategic mating choices are all part of these initiatives. Farmers can more effectively plan lambing and mating schedules by synchronizing the heat cycles of their sheep with controlled mating systems, such as synchronized breeding. Additionally, superior genetics can be introduced and breeding results can be enhanced using artificial insemination (AI).

Monitoring program efficacy and making educated breeding decisions require keeping thorough records of breeding dates, ram utilization, and lambing results. Reproductive management accuracy is increased when breeding tools such as ultrasonography are used for fetal development assessment and pregnancy identification. Over time, flock production and profitability can be optimized by selecting and breeding superior animals with the use of genetic studies and performance tests.

HANDLING THE LAMBING AND PREGNANCY

It is important to pay close attention to the health, diet, and environmental factors of ewes during pregnancy and lambing. Enough nourishment, including the right amounts of protein, minerals, and vitamins, promotes a healthy fetus and lessens the difficulties associated with lambing. Ensuring optimal maternal health and successful lambing outcomes throughout pregnancy involves tracking sheep body condition scores. Additionally crucial to preventing illness and maximizing lamb survival rates are vaccinations and parasite control initiatives.

Setting up clean, dry bedding, enough room, and appropriate ventilation in lambing facilities makes the environment favorable for lambing. When ewes approach lambing, close observation aids in the early detection of any difficulties, enabling timely intervention if necessary. Helping with difficult births or rectifying misrepresentations during lambing can make a big difference in the health of the flock as a whole and the survival rate of the lambs.

TAKING CARE OF REPRODUCTIVE ISSUES

In sheep farming, sustaining optimal flock fertility and productivity requires addressing reproductive problems. Reproductive infections, abortion, stillbirths, and infertility are frequent problems. Regularly doing reproductive health examinations, such as fertility evaluations and pelvic exams, aids in the early detection and resolution of such problems. Strict adherence to quarantine and biosecurity protocols stops the spread of infectious diseases that can affect an individual's ability to reproduce.

Reducing stress and improving reproductive health can be achieved by putting into practice good nutrition and management techniques, such as controlling parasites and managing grazing. Seeking advice from veterinarians or reproductive specialists can offer significant insights into managing particular reproductive issues, such as hormone imbalances, genetic anomalies, and breeding problems. By putting preventative health measures into place, such as immunization schedules and vaccination programs, reproductive risks are reduced and a flock of sheep is kept healthy and productive.

CHAPTER SIX

ACCOMMODATIONS AND AMENITIES

CREATING USABLE AND EFFECTIVE HOUSING STRUCTURES

The comfort and welfare of the animals should be taken into consideration while building housing structures for sheep farming. First, figure out how many sheep the housing can hold, adding extra for future growth if needed. Select a spot that provides shelter from inclement weather, such as strong winds and intense sunlight. With distinct spaces designated for eating, resting, and lambing, the arrangement should make it simple for handlers and sheep to move around.

Prioritizing ventilation in the design will help to preserve the quality of the air and lower the flock's risk of respiratory problems. Furthermore necessary for the health and productivity of the sheep is enough natural light. During hot seasons, strategically include features like skylights and windows to maximize exposure to sunshine and avoid overheating.

Furthermore, make sure you have enough insulation to control the temperature and use as little energy as possible for heating or cooling.

Efficiency is essential for maximizing available space and resources in home design. Daily activities can be made more efficient by putting in place procedures for feeding, water supply, and waste disposal. To minimize labor costs and provide regular access to necessities, think about putting in automatic feeders and waterers. To ensure functionality and efficiency, evaluate and adjust the house design regularly depending on the size, behavior, and seasonal needs of the flock.

PROVIDING SUFFICIENT AIR AND SHELTER

Sheep need a sufficient amount of shelter to keep out predators and harsh weather. The shelter should have distinct sections for feeding, resting, and lambing, and it should be large enough to fit the entire flock comfortably. Select robust materials that offer insulation to control temperature and can resist weather-related stresses.

To avoid respiratory problems and preserve the quality of the air inside the shelter, proper ventilation is essential. Include apertures for windows, vents, or movable panels to let air circulate while keeping the sheep out of the draft. Steer clear of crowding, as this can impede airflow and raise the possibility of diseases spreading across the flock.

For the sheep to live in a healthy environment, the shelter needs to be cleaned and maintained regularly. Take out any collected waste, change the bedding as needed, and look for wear and damage on the structure. Establish a regular cleaning and disinfection regimen to reduce the number of diseases and parasites that spread.

MAINTAINING HYGIENE AND CLEANLINESS

To stop disease outbreaks and improve general health, sheep husbandry must maintain strict cleanliness and hygiene standards. To reduce the danger of contamination, start by implementing stringent handling, feeding, and waste management procedures.

To promote the sheep's development and immune system, give them access to clean water and wholesome nutrition.

Examine the flock frequently for indications of disease or parasites, and address any problems right once to stop them from getting worse. Adhere to the immunization schedule that veterinarians advise to guard against common illnesses. To avoid spreading illnesses, quarantine and examine newcomers before integrating them into the main flock.

When handling sheep or their surroundings, dress appropriately in protective clothing, such as boots and gloves, to maintain proper hygiene. To avoid cross-contamination, keep tools and equipment clean and sterilized.

To stop the transmission of infections, teach employees and handlers good hygiene habits and promote frequent handwashing.

HANDLING TRASH AND ITS EFFECT ON THE ENVIRONMENT

To reduce environmental impact and keep the flock's environment clean and healthy, sheep farming requires effective waste management. Install a waste disposal system that distinguishes between liquid and solid waste, such as urine, and solid waste like manure and bedding. Compost solid waste to create organic fertilizer that can be sold to farmers and gardeners or applied to land.

To reduce methane emissions and turn organic waste into renewable energy, think about installing a biogas digester. Handle waste storage area runoff appropriately to avoid soil erosion and water pollution. Put into effect techniques for conserving soil, such as creating buffer zones beside streams and growing cover crops.

Keep an eye out for leaks or overflows in waste storage facilities and take quick action to resolve any problems that are found. Observe regional laws and environmental guidelines when it comes to disposing of and managing waste. To lessen the farm's environmental impact, teach employees and stakeholders about sustainable practices and promote involvement in recycling and conservation initiatives.

PUTTING SAFETY PROCEDURES IN PLACE FOR HANDLERS AND LIVESTOCK

Sheep farming places a high priority on safety to prevent mishaps and injuries that could harm the animals or their workers. Begin by carrying out a comprehensive risk assessment of the agricultural setting and identifying potential dangers such as electrical equipment, uneven terrain, and sharp items. Put safety procedures into place and train employees and handlers on safe handling methods and emergency protocols.

Make sure that every piece of machinery and infrastructure, including gates, pens, and handling chutes, is in good operating order and is routinely inspected for potential safety risks. To designate danger areas and emergency exits, use the proper signage and markings.

Give handlers personal protection equipment (PPE) such as boots, helmets, and gloves, and make sure they wear them when performing risky duties.

To avoid trips, falls, and slips, keep your workspace tidy and orderly. Keep dangerous goods, pharmaceuticals, and chemicals out of the reach of animals and handling areas. Create and rehearse evacuation plans and emergency response protocols for situations like fires, hurricanes, and disease outbreaks.

Review and update safety procedures regularly in response to comments, events, and operational modifications. To bolster staff and handlers' knowledge and readiness, hold frequent safety meetings and drills. To guarantee a safe and effective working environment for all parties involved in sheep farming operations, give priority to a culture of safety and accountability.

CHAPTER SEVEN

PRACTICES FOR FLOCK MANAGEMENT

CREATING EFFICIENT DOCUMENTATION SYSTEMS

Creating and sustaining efficient record-keeping procedures is a critical component of successful sheep management.

This entails putting important flock-related data in orderly writing, including financial records, immunization schedules, and histories of breeding and lambing as well as individual animal health records.

Create an organized strategy for gathering and archiving data first. For livestock management, use digital spreadsheets or specialized software to keep track of vital information such as dates of birth, weight increases, medical interventions, and breeding cycles. When making management choices, make sure to update these records regularly to guarantee accuracy and accessibility.

Moreover, keep thorough financial records to monitor earnings, outlays, and overall profitability. Feed, veterinary care, equipment, and marketing expenses are included in this.

PUTTING GRAZING AND ROTATION STRATEGIES INTO PRACTICE

Efficient sheep farming techniques require effective grazing and rotation plans. Planning and executing controlled grazing schedules is necessary to maximize pasture growth, reduce soil erosion, and maximize feed consumption.

Start by evaluating the resources in your pasture and separating them into smaller grazing sections, or paddocks. To prevent overgrazing and enable the plants to recover, rotate your flock between paddocks at regular intervals.

Keep an eye on the health of the pasture and modify grazing plans in response to seasonal variations and fodder availability.

To further enhance nutritional intake and diversify your flock's diet, think about implementing mixed-species grazing or using alternative forages. By putting these tactics into practice, sheep farming enterprises can become sustainable and financially successful by increasing flock health and performance as well as pasture health and productivity.

SURVEILLING AND CONTROLLING FLOCK BEHAVIOR

A sustainable and healthy sheep farming enterprise depends on keeping an eye on and controlling flock behavior. This entails watching and comprehending both the dynamics of the flock as a whole as well as the behavior of individual animals.

Begin by keeping a close eye on your flock to spot any unusual behaviors or indicators of stress, disease, or hostility. Learn about the normal behaviors of sheep, including feeding, sleeping, interacting with others, and maintaining the order of the flock.

Use proactive management techniques to resolve behavioral problems and enhance harmonious flock dynamics. This can entail giving people access to enough room, housing, clean water, and nutrient-rich food.

To protect the safety of the flock and the farmer, set up handling and management procedures for aggressive or agitated animals. You may encourage a peaceful and fruitful environment for your sheep by paying close attention to and actively controlling flock behavior.

RECOGNIZING AND RESOLVING PROBLEMS WITH SOCIAL HIERARCHY

Keeping your flock in balance and harmony requires that you recognize and resolve challenges related to social hierarchy. Similar to many other herd animals, sheep use dominance-based interactions and behaviors to create social hierarchies.

To find the dominant and submissive members of the flock, start by watching how they interact with one another. Indicators of problems with social hierarchy such as violence, bullying, or exclusion should be kept an eye out for.

Put these problems into practice by implementing tactics like allocating enough room and resources to lessen rivalry and conflict. To keep other flock members safe, think about temporarily separating dominant or violent animals.

Encourage healthy social connections by observing group dynamics and introducing new animals gradually. Offering diverse feeding alternatives and enrichment activities can also aid in lowering stress levels and fostering a more laid-back social atmosphere among the flock. You may establish a flock that is more harmonious and productive by recognizing and resolving challenges related to social hierarchy.

ORGANIZING FOR WEATHER AND SEASONAL CHANGES

Making informed plans for weather and seasonal variations is essential to maintaining the well-being and productivity of your sheep flock. Seasons present different opportunities and difficulties that call for proactive management techniques.

To begin, familiarize yourself with the local weather and seasonal patterns. Take into account variables including temperature swings, precipitation totals, wind exposure, and the availability of fodder throughout the year.

Create seasonal management plans that handle important issues including providing shelter and bedding during severe weather, modifying feeding schedules by dietary requirements, and putting parasite control methods into action as necessary.

Ample facilities, veterinary assistance, and nutritional supplementation for ewes in pregnancy and lactation should be provided to prepare for the seasonal breeding and lambing seasons. To reduce hazards and maximize flock performance all year long, keep an eye on weather forecasts and be ready to modify management strategies as necessary

CHAPTER EIGHT

STRATEGIES FOR MARKETING AND SALES

RECOGNIZING DEMAND AND MARKET TRENDS

Success in the sheep farming industry depends on having a solid awareness of market trends and demand. To determine the current trends in sheep goods, such as wool, meat, and dairy, extensive market research is first conducted.

You may better customize your sheep farming operations to match market demands by analyzing consumer preferences and wants. For example, you can increase sales and draw in new customers by modifying your farming operations to meet the growing demand for ethically raised meat or organic wool.

Additionally, keeping abreast of market trends enables you to predict shifts in demand and modify your production and marketing plans accordingly. This could entail keeping an eye on rival items, reacting to changes in customer preferences, and tracking seasonal variations in demand. You may maximize the profitability of your sheep farming endeavor, prevent shortages or overstocking, and optimize your output levels by keeping an eye on market trends and swings in demand.

Furthermore, using market data and analytics to inform strategic choices can help with things like product diversification, focusing on specialized markets, and looking for new growth prospects. Sheep producers are more equipped to remain competitive, flexible, and responsive to changing consumer needs thanks to this thorough approach to studying market trends and demand.

CREATING A UNIQUE BRAND IDENTITY FOR YOUR ITEMS

In a crowded market, standing out with your sheep farming products requires strong brand identification. It entails identifying your USPs, which could have to do with the heritage and legend of your sheep breeds, the sustainability of your farming methods, or the caliber of your wool. Developing an engaging brand story that connects with your target market will assist increase product recognition, trust, and loyalty.

Moreover, creating a brand identity includes designing visual components like packaging, promotional materials, and logos. These components must be in line with the principles of your brand and appeal to the tastes of your intended audience. To attract environmentally sensitive customers, you can use eco-friendly packaging for wool items or highlight your farm's moral business practices in marketing materials.

Furthermore, maintaining a consistent brand identity throughout all touchpoints—including web, physical stores, and promotional events—reinforces your brand identification and increases customer memory. Developing a distinctive brand identity helps you stand out from the competition and make a lasting impression on consumers.

INVESTIGATING SALES AND MARKETING CHANNELS

To reach your target audience and increase sales of your sheep farming products, you must implement effective marketing and sales methods. By investigating several marketing channels, you may reach consumers via a variety of touchpoints, boosting exposure and interaction.

This could involve offline channels like farmer's markets, specialized shops, and partnerships with nearby companies, as well as internet channels including e-commerce platforms, social media marketing, and email advertising.

Leveraging sales opportunities also entails figuring out when sheep items sell best, such as during wool festivals, holiday promotions, or agricultural shows. Engaging in these occasions and making the most of marketing initiatives at busy times can greatly increase revenue and attract new clients. Furthermore, forming alliances with distributors, wholesalers, or retailers broadens your market penetration.

Additionally, implementing omnichannel marketing techniques that smoothly combine offline and online platforms improves consumer ease and involvement. This might entail setting up virtual farm tours or workshops, allowing in-store pickup for online orders, and offering individualized customer service.

Sheep producers may optimize their visibility, sales conversion, and customer happiness by investigating a variety of marketing platforms and sales prospects.

COST ANALYSIS AND PRICING STRATEGIES

Running a profitable sheep farming business requires careful cost analysis and the development of effective pricing strategies. Keeping your prices competitive and profitable means knowing how consumers view your items' worth, production costs, and market conditions. Finding the true costs of sheep farming, such as feed costs, labor, veterinary care, equipment maintenance, and overhead expenses, is made easier by performing a cost analysis.

In addition, the assessment of pricing strategies takes into account many elements like pricing elasticity, competition pricing, cost-plus pricing, value-based pricing, and product differentiation. Bulk meat sales may profit from volume-based pricing methods, whereas premium wool goods may command higher prices because of their superior quality and distinctive features.

Additionally, regular cost-benefit evaluations aid in maximizing resource allocation, spotting chances for cost savings, and raising overall productivity in sheep farming operations.

This could entail calculating the return on investment (ROI) for different farming techniques, equipment improvements, advertising campaigns, and business growth plans. Sheep producers can attain sustainable profitability and financial success through the use of effective pricing strategies and well-informed cost research.

DEVELOPING LOYALTY AND RELATIONSHIPS WITH CUSTOMERS

Establishing enduring bonds with clients and encouraging allegiance are critical to sheep farming's long-term success. It all begins with giving customers the best possible experiences, from dependable and high-quality products to individualized assistance and care. You may successfully grasp the wants, preferences, and feedback of your customers by interacting with them through social media platforms, surveys, and feedback methods.

Additionally, putting in place customer loyalty plans, discounts, and awards promotes recurring business and brand promotion among current clients. This could include special offerings, referral schemes, membership perks, or discounts for devoted clients.

Developing a feeling of belonging and community around your business improves client retention and stimulates good word-of-mouth advertising.

Additionally, you may cultivate trust, contentment, and loyalty by actively listening to customer input, swiftly addressing problems, and consistently upgrading your products and services based on customer insights. In addition to open communication, moral business conduct, and sincere involvement that is consistent with your brand values, developing long-term relationships with customers also requires several other elements. Sheep farmers who prioritize client connections and loyalty can build a devoted customer base, encourage repeat business, and maintain business growth.

CHAPTER NINE

MONEY HANDLING

SETTING ASIDE MONEY FOR STARTUP AND ONGOING EXPENSES

Budgeting is essential for assuring both financial stability and success when beginning a sheep farming business. Start by enumerating every cost involved in establishing and operating a sheep farm. This covers buying or renting property, getting sheep, erecting fences and shelters, procuring feeding supplies and shearing gear, and paying for the first round of veterinary bills. To determine reasonable expenses, find out what these things are selling for on the market.

Next, draft a thorough budget that details your anticipated costs and revenue for the first year or more of business. Take into account seasonal variances, such as higher feeding expenses in the winter or possible swings in the market pricing of meat and wool. Take into account extra expenses for marketing, labor, and continuing veterinarian care.

It's critical to forecast conservatively to accommodate for unforeseen costs and lower-than-anticipated revenue.

Review your budget frequently and make any necessary adjustments depending on your actual income and expenses. You'll be able to manage your finances better and make wise choices regarding the expansion of your company and the distribution of your resources. Keep in mind that creating an efficient budget involves more than just lowering expenses—it also entails making smart investments in areas that will support your sheep farming company's long-term development.

MONITORING REVENUE AND EXPENSES

An essential component of financial management in sheep farming is keeping track of income and expenses. To keep track of all the financial activities associated with your farm, such as purchases, sales of animals or goods like wool, feed costs, veterinary bills, equipment upkeep, and other connected activities, use accounting software or spreadsheets.

Sort these transactions into categories to see a clear picture of your money's origins and destinations.

Make sure your financial records are accurate by regularly reconciling them to find any inconsistencies or possible areas for improvement. This will assist you in making well-informed choices on pricing policies, cost-cutting techniques, and resource allocation. Maintain thorough records of all of your revenue streams, including lamb, wool, and other product sales, and use trend analysis to predict future revenue streams.

You can get a thorough grasp of the financial situation of your farm by keeping meticulous records of your income and expenses. Making strategic decisions, seeing growth prospects, and guaranteeing the long-term viability of the sheep farming industry all benefit greatly from this knowledge.

PUTTING RISK MANAGEMENT AND FINANCIAL CONTROLS IN PLACE

To minimize potential problems and guarantee the financial stability of your sheep farming endeavor, you must implement financial controls and risk management procedures. Establish explicit financial policies and procedures first, such as regular financial reporting schedules, restrictions on authorized spending, and processes for budget approval. This promotes accountability inside your company and helps avoid overpaying.

Determine the possible threats to your farm's finances, such as shifting feed or livestock market prices, illness outbreaks among your sheep, or unforeseen weather events that affect output.

Create backup plans and risk-reduction techniques to deal with these issues ahead of time. This could entail creating an emergency fund to meet unforeseen costs, getting insurance coverage for important possessions, or diversifying your sources of income.

Examine your financial results regularly in comparison to benchmarks and key performance indicators (KPIs) to evaluate how well your risk management and financial controls are working.

Modify your plans as necessary in response to shifting market conditions or internal issues that have an impact on the profitability of your farm. Establishing strong risk management procedures and financial controls will make you more equipped to handle unforeseen circumstances and succeed in sheep farming in the long run.

LOOKING FOR INVESTMENT AND FINANCING POSSIBILITIES

Getting money and looking into investment possibilities might provide your sheep farming business with the resources it needs to survive and expand. Begin by determining possible funding sources, including agricultural grants, loans from farming-focused financial institutions, and joint ventures with other industry players. To select the best solution for your needs, do some research and comparison shopping for terms and conditions.

Create a thorough business plan that details the goals, financial forecasts, and expansion strategy for your farm. This paper is essential for drawing in possible lenders or investors by showcasing your capacity to create returns on investment, understand the market, and have a clear goal. Emphasize your farm's distinctive selling features, such as its superior goods, sustainable methods, or creative shearing techniques.

Get involved with regional agricultural associations, governmental organizations, and business associations to learn about funding sources, industry gatherings, and sheep farmer-specific networking opportunities. Develop connections with possible partners or investors by demonstrating your knowledge, openness, and dedication to moral agricultural methods. To bolster your funding requests, be ready to include risk analyses, cash flow forecasts, and financial statements.

ORGANIZING FOR FINANCIAL SUSTAINABILITY OVER THE LONG TERM

Sheep farming needs proactive decision-making, ongoing monitoring, and strategic planning to be financially sustainable over the long run.

Create a long-term financial plan that fits the objectives, principles, and market conditions of your farm. This could entail adding new products to your line, looking into specialized markets, or implementing eco-friendly procedures that appeal to customers who care about the environment to diversify your sources of income.

Make investments in infrastructure and technology upgrades to increase output, lower operating costs, and improve efficiency on your farm.

To maximize resource utilization and reduce waste, this can entail making investments in automated feeding systems, renewable energy sources, or precision farming methods. Make sure these activities are helping your bottom line by routinely assessing their return on investment.

Keep an eye on customer preferences, market trends, and legislative developments that can affect the sheep farming sector. In a market that is constantly changing, stay up to date on new technology, industry standards, and best practices to maintain your competitive edge.

To ensure long-term financial sustainability and success in sheep farming, continually evaluate and modify your financial plans in light of new opportunities, risks, and performance indicators.

CHAPTER TEN

SUSTAINABILITY OF THE ENVIRONMENT

PUTTING SUSTAINABLE FARMING PRACTICES INTO PRACTICE

The long-term sustainability of sheep farming operations depends on the adoption of sustainable farming practices. This entails a variety of tactics designed to reduce environmental effects while preserving output.

Soil management, which includes techniques like rotational grazing to stop soil erosion and enhance soil health, is one important component. Composting and the use of organic fertilizers both contribute to soil fertility maintenance without the need for artificial chemicals.

Water management is another essential component of sustainable farming. This entails minimizing water waste, collecting rainwater, and installing effective irrigation systems.

Farmers may save costs and conserve water by employing water-efficient equipment and adopting water-saving strategies like drip irrigation. Furthermore, limiting energy consumption using renewable energy sources, such as solar panels, can help the farm leave less of an environmental impact.

EFFECTIVELY MANAGING RESOURCES (WATER, ENERGY, ETC.)

Sustainable sheep husbandry depends on effective resource management. This covers energy, water, and other resources that are essential to farming operations. Water management techniques include things like putting in water-saving fixtures, collecting and reusing rainwater, and setting up water-efficient irrigation systems. Farmers may minimize expenses and lessen their impact on the environment by managing their water use.

In a similar vein, sustainable farming depends on effective energy management. This entails making use of energy-saving devices, funding the purchase of renewable energy sources like solar or wind power, and putting energy-saving measures in place such as appropriate insulation and lighting controls. Farmers may help conserve the environment and lessen their carbon footprint by consuming less energy and relying less on fossil fuels.

ENCOURAGING ECOSYSTEM HEALTH AND BIODIVERSITY

Encouraging biodiversity and the well-being of ecosystems is fundamental to successful sheep husbandry. This entails establishing wildlife-friendly zones on the farm, planting native plants, and protecting natural ecosystems. Farmers may help pollinators, beneficial insects, and wildlife, all of which contribute to a balanced environment and increase agricultural resilience, by increasing biodiversity.

Furthermore, using integrated pest management (IPM) strategies encourages natural pest control mechanisms and lessens the need for chemical pesticides. To properly manage pest populations, this involves importing beneficial insects, rotating crops, and utilizing biological controls. Farmer sustainability can be improved and environmental impact can be decreased by preserving a healthy ecosystem.

TAKING ON THE CHALLENGES OF CLIMATE CHANGE

Modern sheep husbandry faces many issues, one of which is addressing the effects of climate change. By using carbon sequestration techniques like cover crops, rotational grazing, and agroforestry, farmers can lessen the effects of climate change. By enhancing soil health and removing carbon dioxide from the atmosphere, these methods aid in mitigating and adapting to climate change.

Farmers can also better adapt to changing climate conditions by implementing climate-smart agricultural practices, such as drought-resistant crop types, water-efficient irrigation, and heat-tolerant livestock breeds. Farmers may distribute risk and lessen their exposure to catastrophic weather occurrences by diversifying their livestock and crops, which will also ensure the long-term stability of their farming operations.

TAKING PART IN CONSERVATION PROGRAMS

Being proactive in conservation efforts is one way to practice sustainable sheep husbandry. To carry out conservation projects including habitat restoration, watershed protection, and wildlife conservation, farmers can work with conservation organizations, governmental organizations, and neighborhood associations.

Farmers can benefit their farms and the environment by actively participating in conservation projects that support ecosystem restoration and biodiversity conservation.

Furthermore, implementing environmentally friendly certification schemes and upholding environmental standards can improve the farm's standing, draw in eco-aware customers, and create new business prospects.

Farmers can position themselves as leaders in sustainable agriculture and stewards of the land, promoting a good impact on the environment and society, by showcasing their dedication to sustainability and conservation.

CHAPTER ELEVEN

UPCOMING DEVELOPMENTS AND TRENDS

EXAMINING THE USE OF TECHNOLOGY IN SHEEP FARMING

Technology is a key component of modern sheep husbandry, helping to increase productivity and efficiency. The adoption of electronic identification systems (EID) for individual sheep is one important component. EID tags have distinct identification numbers that can be read by automated systems or handheld devices. Farmers can accurately track each sheep's health, breeding history, and productivity data thanks to this technology. Furthermore, it is possible to combine automatic feeding systems, which guarantee that sheep are fed at the proper times and in the right amounts, minimizing waste and labor expenses.

Precision farm tools are another technological advancement that is transforming sheep farming. These include sensors that track pasture quality, soil moisture content, and environmental factors, as well as drones with GPS capability. Farmers can find possible risks or opportunities for improvement by using drones to examine grazing fields from the air. Precise fertilization plans are made possible by the real-time data on nutrient levels provided by soil sensors. With the use of these tools, farmers can make data-driven decisions that improve yields and resource management.

Furthermore, sheep farming's breeding methods have changed as a result of developments in reproductive technology including artificial insemination (AI) and embryo transfer. With artificial intelligence (AI), farmers can obtain superior genetics without having to have a sizable ram flock. Through the use of surrogate ewes, embryo transfer techniques amplify elite genetics, enabling rapid genetic improvement. These innovations hasten the process of breeding, creating herds of sheep that are healthier and more fruitful.

USING ORGANIC AND SUSTAINABLE PRACTICES

Sheep farming is changing to use more organic and sustainable methods in response to consumer demand for goods that are made ethically and sustainably. Using rotational grazing techniques for pasture management is one crucial component. Sheep are rotated between smaller paddocks within pastures through the use of rotational grazing techniques. Through the enhancement of organic matter and nutrient cycling, this method reduces overgrazing, encourages grass regeneration, and enhances soil health.

Integrated pest management (IPM), which lessens the need for chemical pesticides, is another sustainable approach. Using trap crops, reintroducing natural predators, and adopting cultural practices like crop rotation are examples of IPM tactics. Farmers preserve the ecological balance of their crops and safeguard vital insects and pollinators by using fewer pesticides.

Furthermore, the requirements for organic certification push farmers to use comprehensive management techniques. These include staying away from artificial chemicals, utilizing organic feed and forage, giving animal welfare a top priority, and putting biodiversity conservation strategies into action. High-quality meat and wool are produced by organic sheep farming, which also supports sustainable land management and environmental preservation.

MONITORING INNOVATIONS AND INDUSTRY TRENDS

For sheep farming operations to be successful, staying current with developments and trends in the sector is essential. The growing need for high-end and specialized wool products is one trend. Customers are prepared to pay more for wool clothing that is sustainable, traceable, and produced ethically. This trend offers sheep farmers the chance to concentrate on producing wool of the highest caliber and putting optimal practices in place for processing and producing wool.

The emergence of specialized markets for products like organic and grass-fed lamb is another trend. Organic and pasture-raised lamb products are growing more popular as consumers become more aware of the effects that their purchases have on the environment, animal welfare, and food quality. By using pasture-based agricultural methods, certifying their goods as organic, and targeting health-conscious consumers directly, farmers can profit from this trend.

Additionally, sheep farmers now have additional ways to connect with consumers because of advancements in marketing and distribution methods. Online marketplaces, farmers' markets, farm-to-table eateries, and specialty shops offer chances to present distinctive goods and establish direct connections with customers. Businesses engaged in sheep farming can stand out in a crowded market by utilizing branding initiatives, narrative techniques, and digital marketing strategies.

PROSPECTS FOR GROWTH AND DIVERSIFICATION

In sheep farming, diversification and expansion are calculated strategies for optimizing profits and reducing risks. Value-added goods like wool crafts, artisanal cheeses, lamb sausages, and natural healthcare products present one opportunity. By adding value to items made from sheep, farmers can increase their profit margins and provide distinctive products to target niche markets.

Agrotourism and farm experiences are another way to broaden your portfolio. Providing guided tours, educational workshops, farm stays, and agritourism events to the public can create new revenue streams and boost rural tourism on farms. Public education about sheep farming encourages community involvement, strengthens brand loyalty, and gives guests experiences they won't soon forget.

Additionally, investigating cooperative alliances and supply chain integration may present chances for vertical integration. Creating synergies throughout the sheep farming value chain can be achieved by collaborating with regional textile mills, shops, chefs, and artisans. For instance, partnering with a restaurant to highlight lamb dishes or working with a wool spinner to create special yarn mixes can build mutually beneficial relationships and broaden market reach.

ONGOING EDUCATION AND TALENT ACQUISITION

To succeed in the ever-changing world of sheep farming, one must always be learning new things and developing their skills. Programs for further education and training provided by colleges, industry associations, and agricultural extension services might be advantageous to farmers. Sheep nutrition, health management, breeding methods, pasture management, business planning, and marketing strategies are a few possible topics.

Furthermore, networking with other farmers, going to conferences, and taking part in workshops are excellent ways to learn from peers, share expertise, and remain current with industry practices. Establishing a strong network of mentors, advisors, and specialists can provide direction and understanding to overcome obstacles and take advantage of new opportunities.

Additionally, using digital tools and technology to manage farms, keep records, analyze data, and make decisions improves production and operational efficiency. Convenient alternatives to obtain specialized training and resources catering to the needs of sheep farming include online courses, webinars, and e-learning platforms. Farmers who pursue continuous learning are better equipped to adjust to shifting market conditions, implement cutting-edge techniques, and maintain sheep farming's long-term viability.

www.ingramcontent.com/pod-product-compliance
Lightning Source LLC
Chambersburg PA
CBHW071838210526
45479CB00001B/192